Anglo-American Cataloguing Rules

SECOND EDITION

Chapter 9
Computer Files
DRAFT REVISION

Edited, for the Joint Steering
Committee for Revision of AACR,
by Michael Gorman

AMERICAN LIBRARY ASSOCIATION Chicago and London
CANADIAN LIBRARY ASSOCIATION Ottawa
THE LIBRARY ASSOCIATION London   1987

Library of Congress Cataloging-in-Publication Data

Anglo-American cataloguing rules. 9. Computer files.
   Anglo-American cataloguing rules, second edition.
Chapter 9, Computer files (draft revision).

   Revision of the chapter originally titled: Machine-
readable data files.
   1. Cataloging of machine-readable data files--Rules.
2. Descriptive cataloging--Rules.   I. Gorman, Michael,
1941-   . II. Joint Steering Committee for Revision of
AACR.   III. American Library Association.   IV. Anglo-
American cataloguing rules. 9. Machine-readable data files.
Z695.615.A46 1987   025.3'49   87-1052
ISBN 0-8389-3339-4

British Library Cataloguing in Publication Data

Anglo-American cataloguing rules second edition : chapter
   9 : computer files : draft revision.
   1. Cataloging of machine-readable data files
   I. Gorman, Michael, 1941- II. Anglo-American cataloging
   rules
   025.3'49   Z695.47
   ISBN 0-85365-568-5

Preface

The Joint Steering Committee for Revision of the Anglo-American Cataloguing Rules (JSCAACR) has recommended that this preliminary draft of a revision of the rules for the descriptive cataloguing of computer files be published to help bridge the gap between the rules a library may be using now -- the rules for the descriptive cataloguing of machine-readable files published as Chapter 9 of the Anglo-American Cataloguing Rules, second edition (AACR2) or Guidelines for Using AACR2 Chapter 9 for Cataloging Microcomputer Software (Chicago: ALA, 1984) or Study of Cataloguing Computer Software: Applying AACR2 to Microcomputer Programs ([London]: British Library, 1984) -- and the eventual publication of the final version in 1988.

A study of the three earlier works was a starting point for the discussions and resultant decisions found in this document. Input received from the Working Group on the International Standard Bibliographic Description for Computer Files was also considered.

It must be emphasized that this is a preliminary draft of the rules for computer files. This draft has yet to be checked for consistency with other parts of AACR2 and to undergo the usual editorial process. The final version, to be included in AACR2 consolidated, scheduled to be published in 1988, will probably contain changes in detail. No changes in concept will be made.

The proposed revised rule for accompanying materials in AACR2 Chapter 1 have been added as an addendum to assist in understanding the changes demonstrated in some Chapter 9 examples. This rule is also subject to changes in detail.

Comments and suggestions are always welcome and should be addressed to the appropriate constituent body represented on JSCAACR.

JEAN WEIHS, Chairperson
Joint Steering Committee for Revision of AACR

Contents

Contents

Chapter 9
Computer Files

9.0. GENERAL RULES

9.0A. Scope

The rules in this chapter cover the description of
files that are encoded for manipulation by computer.
These files comprise data and programs. Computer files
may be stored on, or contained in, carriers available
for direct access or by remote access.

The rules in this chapter do not cover electronic
devices such as calculators, etc.; see Chapter 10 for
such materials. Programs residing in the permanent
memory of a computer (ROM) or firmware are considered
to be part of the device and should be described in
conjunction with the device (e.g., the programming
language of a particular computer, such as: Applesoft
in ROM).

9.0B. Sources of information

9.0B1. Chief source of information. The chief source
of information for computer files is the title
screen(s). If the item being described consists of two
or more separate physical parts, treat a container or
its permanently affixed label that is the unifying ele-
ment as the chief source of information if it furnishes
a collective title and the formally presented information in, or the labels on, the parts themselves do not.
If there is no title screen, take the information from
other formally presented internal evidence (main menus,
program statements, etc.).

If the information required is not available[1] from internal sources, take it from the following sources (in this order of preference):

the physical carrier or its labels[2]
information (in printed or computer-readable form) issued by the publisher, creator, etc., with the file (commonly called "documentation")
information printed on the container issued by the publisher, distributor, etc.

In case of variance between fullness of information found in these sources, prefer the source with the most complete information. If the information required is not available (see footnote 1) from the chief source or the sources listed above, take it from the following sources (in this order of preference):

other published descriptions of the file
other sources

9.0B2. Prescribed sources of information. The prescribed source(s) of information for each area of the description of computer files is set out below. Enclose information taken from outside the prescribed source(s) in square brackets.

AREA	PRESCRIBED SOURCES OF INFORMATION
Title and statement of responsibility	Chief source of information, the carrier or its labels, information issued by the publisher, creator, etc., container

---

1. <u>Available</u>, in this context, includes the cataloguer's access to equipment to mount or read the file.

2. By <u>label</u> is meant any permanently affixed paper, plastic, etc., label that is added by the publisher, creator, etc., of the file, as opposed to those added locally, and as opposed to the container itself, which may have data embossed or printed on it.

AREA	PRESCRIBED SOURCES OF INFORMATION
Edition	Chief source of information, the carrier or its labels, information issued by the publisher, creator, etc., container
File characteristics	Any source
Publication, distribution, etc.	Chief source of information, the carrier or its labels, information issued by the publisher, creator, etc., container
Physical description	Any source
Series	Chief source of information, the carrier or its labels, information issued by the publisher, creator, etc., container
Note	Any source
Standard number and terms of availability	Any source

9.0C. Punctuation

For the punctuation of the description as a whole, see 1.0C.

For the prescribed punctuation of elements, see the following rules.

9.0D. Levels of detail in the description

See 1.0D.

9.0E. Language and script of the description

See 1.0E.

9.0F. Inaccuracies

See 1.0F.

3

9.0G. Accents and other diacritical marks
See 1.0G.

9.0H. Items with several chief sources of information
See 1.0H.

9.1. TITLE AND STATEMENT OF RESPONSIBILITY AREA

Contents:
9.1A.   Preliminary rule
9.1B.   Title proper
9.1C.   General material designation
9.1D.   Parallel titles
9.1E.   Other title information
9.1F.   Statements of responsibility
9.1G.   Items without a collective title

9.1A. Preliminary rule

9.1A1. Punctuation
For instructions on the use of spaces before and after prescribed punctuation, see 1.0C.

Precede the title of a supplement or section (see 1.1B9) by a full stop.

Enclose the general material designation in square brackets.

Precede each parallel title by an equals sign.

Precede each unit of other title information by a colon.

Precede the first statement of responsibility by a diagonal slash.

Precede each subsequent statement of responsibility by a semicolon.

For the punctuation of this area for items without a collective title, see 1.1G.

9.1B. Title proper

9.1B1. Record the title proper as instructed in 1.1B.

WordStar

Practicalc II

Demon attack

The CPS 1974 American national election survey

Krell's Logo

Visitrend + Visiplot

Record the source of the title proper in a note (see 9.7B3).

9.1B2. Do not record a file name or a data set name as the title proper unless it is the <u>only</u> name given in the chief source. If desired, give a file name or data set name not used as the title proper in a note (see 9.7B4).

9.1B3. If no title can be found in any source, devise a brief descriptive title (see 1.1B7) and enclose it in square brackets. Indicate in a note that the title has been supplied (see 9.7B3).

[Library catalogue, 1969-1975]
<u>Note</u>: Title supplied by cataloguer

9.1C. <u>Optional addition.</u> **General material designation**

9.1C1. Add immediately following the title proper the appropriate general material designation as instructed in 1.1C.

VIEW [GMD]

Gertrude's puzzles [GMD]

[Add "computer file" to, and delete "machine-readable data file" from, both lists in 1.1C1.]

9.1C2. If an item contains parts belonging to materials falling into two or more categories, and if none of these is the predominant constituent of the item, give either <u>multimedia</u> or <u>kit</u> as the designation (see 1.1C1 and 1.10).

9.1D. **Parallel titles**

9.1D1. Record parallel titles as instructed in 1.1D.

5

Citizen participation in non-work-time activities [GMD] = Participation des citoyens aux activités hors des heures de travail

El Asistente del instructor [GMD] = Teaching assistant

9.1E.   Other title information

9.1E1.   Record other title information as instructed in 1.1E.

Vufile [GMD] : an information retrieval system for use with files, lists, and data bases of all kinds

A.C.E. [GMD] : Applesoft command editor

Political participation in five sections of Milan [GMD] = La partecipazione politica e associative in cinque quartieri di Milano : Baffio, Barona, Comasine, Forlanini, Perrucchetti

9.1F.   Statements of responsibility

9.1F1.   Record statements of responsibility relating to those persons or bodies responsible for the content of the file as instructed in 1.1F.

Database [GMD] / Paul Fellows

VIEW [GMD] / Protechnic Computers Ltd.

The China study [GMD] / principal investigator, Angus Campbell

Memory castle [GMD] / designed by Donna Stanger ; programmed by Lon Koenig

Class records system [GMD] / by Quercus

Give statements relating to collaborators, sponsors, etc., or to persons or bodies who have prepared or contributed to the production of the file, in a note (see 9.7B6).

9.1F2. Add a word or short phrase to the statement of responsibility if the relationship between the title of the work and the person(s) or body (bodies) named in the statement is not clear.

> A reconstruction of Oliver Benson's "Simple diplomatic game" [GMD] / [developed by] Jeff Krend

> Redistricting program [GMD] / [prepared by] Stuart Nagel [for the] Inter-university Consortium for Political Research

9.1G. Items without a collective title

9.1G1. If an item lacks a collective title, record the titles of the individual parts as instructed in 1.1G.

> Personal bibliographic system / by Victor Rosenberg. Data transfer system / written by Cyrus Galambor and Peter Rycus [GMD]

> Let's go to a beer bust / written by Sue Beall and Wayne Wyllie ; programmed by Kathy Kothmann. Time out / written by Ruth Cady ; programmed by Kathy Kothmann. Blood alcohol content / by Robert S. Gold [GMD]

9.1G2. Make the relationship between statements of responsibility and the parts of an item lacking a collective title clear by additions as instructed in 9.1F2.

9.2. EDITION AREA

Contents:
9.2A. Preliminary rule
9.2B. Edition statement
9.2C. Statements of responsibility relating to the edition
9.2D. Subsequent edition statement
9.2E. Statements of responsibility relating to a subsequent edition statement

9.2A. Preliminary rule

9.2A1. Punctuation

For instructions on the use of spaces before and after prescribed punctuation, see 1.0C.

Precede this area by a full stop, space, dash, space.

Precede a subsequent edition statement by a comma.

Precede the first statement of responsibility following an edition or subsequent edition statement by a diagonal slash.

Precede each subsequent statement of responsibility by a semicolon.

9.2B. Edition statement

9.2B1. Transcribe a statement relating to a named reissue of a computer file, or to an edition of the file that contains differences from other editions, as instructed in 1.2B.

Rev. ed.

NORC test ed.

Level 3.4

Rev. ed. 10/2/82

3rd update

Version 5.20

[Version] 1.1

Prelim. release 0.5

Record the source of the edition statement in a note (see 9.7B7) if it is different from that of the title proper.

9.2B2. In case of doubt about whether a statement is an edition statement, take the presence of words such as edition, issue, version, release, level, update (or their equivalents in other languages) as evidence that the statement is an edition statement, and record it as such.

9.2B3. Optional addition. If the file lacks an edition

statement but is known to contain significant changes from other editions (e.g., changes in the data involving content, standardized coding, etc.; changes in the programming including changes in the program statements, programming language, and programming routines and operations; the addition of sound or graphics; improvement of graphics), supply a suitable brief statement in the language and script of the title proper and enclose it in square brackets.

[Version 7]

9.2B4. Do not treat an issue of a file which incorporates minor changes as a new edition. Such minor changes include corrections of misspellings of data, changes in the arrangement of the contents, changes in the output format or the display medium, and changes in the physical characteristics (blocking factors, recording density, etc.). If desired, give the details of such changes in a note (see 9.7B7).

9.2B5. Record an edition statement appearing in accompanying material only if it also refers to the file. In cases of doubt, do not record such an edition statement.

9.2B6. If an edition statement appears in more than one language or script, record the statement that is in the language or script of the title proper. If this criterion does not apply, record the statement that appears first. <u>Optionally</u>, give the parallel statements, each preceded by an equals sign.

9.2B7. If an item lacking a collective title and is described as a unit contains one or more parts with an associated edition statement, record such statements following the titles and statements of responsibility to which they relate, separated from them by a full stop.

9.2C. **Statements of responsibility relating to the edition**

9.2C1. Record a statement of responsibility relating to one or more editions, but not to all editions, of a file as instructed in 1.2C and 9.1F. If desired, give other statements of responsibility relating to the edition in a note (see 9.7B7).

> Rev. ed. / program has been converted from BASIC to FORTRAN IV by Allen P. Smith

9.2D. Subsequent edition statement

9.2D1. If the item is a named revision of a particular edition containing changes from that edition, give the subsequent edition statement as instructed in 1.2D.

> ICPSR ed., OSIRIS IV version

Do not record statements relating to subsequent issues of a file when the changes are of a minor nature (see 9.2B4).

9.2E. Statements of responsibility relating to a subsequent edition statement

9.2E1. Record a statement of responsibility relating to one or more designated subsequent revisions (but not to all subsequent revisions) of a particular edition, as instructed in 1.2C and 9.1F.

> 3rd ed., Version 1.2 / programmed by W.G. Toepfer

9.3. FILE CHARACTERISTICS AREA

Contents:
9.3A. Preliminary rule
9.3B. File characteristics

9.3A. Preliminary rule

9.3A1. Punctuation

For instructions on the use of spaces before and after prescribed punctuation, see 1.0C.
Precede this area by a full stop, space, dash, space.
Enclose each statement of the number of records, statements, etc., in parentheses.
Precede a statement of the number of records, statements, etc., by a colon when that number follows the number of files.

9.3B. File characteristics

9.3B1. Designation. When the information is readily available, indicate the type of file. Use one of the following terms:

> Computer data

> Computer program(s)

> Computer data and program(s)

Optionally, if general material designations are used (see 9.1C), omit the word "computer" from the file designation.

9.3B2. Number of records, statements, etc. If a file designation is given and if the information is readily available, record the number or approximate number of files that make up the content (use "file" or "files" preceded by an arabic numeral) and/or these other details:

a) Data. Give the number or approximate number of records and/or bytes;

> Computer data (1 file : 350 records)

> Computer data (2 files)

> Computer data (550 records)

> Computer data (1 file : 600 records, 2400 bytes)

b) Programs. Give the number or approximate number of statements and/or bytes;

> Computer program (1 file : 200 statements)

> Computer program (2150 statements)

> Computer programs (2 files : 4300, 1250 bytes)

c) Multipart files. Give the number or approximate number of records and/or bytes or statements and/or bytes in each part.

Computer data (3 files : 100, 460, 550 records

Computer program (2 files : ca. 330 statements each)

Computer data (2 files : 800, 1250 records) and programs (3 files : 7260, 3490, 5076 bytes)

If such numbering cannot be given succinctly, omit the information from this area. If desired, give it in a note (see 9.7B8).

9.4. PUBLICATION, DISTRIBUTION, ETC., AREA

Contents:
9.4A. Preliminary rule
9.4B. General rule
9.4C. Place of publication, distribution, etc.
9.4D. Name of publisher, distributor, etc.
9.4E. Statement of function of publisher, distributor, etc.
9.4F. Date of publication, distribution, etc.

9.4A. Preliminary rule

9.4A1. Punctuation

For instructions on the use of spaces before and after prescribed punctuation, see 1.0C.
Precede this area by a full stop, space, dash, space.
Precede a second or subsequently named place of publication, distribution, etc., by a semicolon.
Precede the name of a publisher, distributor, etc., by a colon.
Enclose a supplied statement of function of a publisher, distributor, etc., in square brackets.
Precede the date of publication, distribution, etc., by a comma.

9.4B. General rule
For items with multiple places and names of publishers, distributors, etc., follow the instructions in 1.4B.

9.4C. Place of publication, distribution, etc.

9.4C1. Record the place of publication, distribution, etc., of a published computer file as instructed in 1.4C.

9.4C2. Do not record a place of publication, distribution, etc., of an unpublished computer file. Do not record s.l. in such a case.

9.4D. Name of publisher, distributor, etc.

9.4D1. Record the name of the publisher, distributor, etc., of a published computer file as instructed in 1.4D.

> London : Psion
>
> Newton Upper Falls, Mass. ; Ipswich : Practicorp
> (For a cataloguing agency in the United
> Kingdom)
>
> Prague : [s.n.]
>
> [S.l.] : Bruce & James Program Publishers ;
> [Distributed by Simon & Schuster]
>
> Bellevue, Wash. : Temporal Acuity Products ;
> Owatonna, Minn. : Distributed exclusively by
> Musictronic

9.4D2. Do not record the name of a publisher, distributor, etc., of an unpublished computer file. Do not record s.n. in such a case.

9.4E. Optional addition. Statement of function of publisher, distributor, etc.

9.4E1. Add to the name of a publisher, distributor, etc., a statement of function as instructed in 1.4E.

> Chicago : National Opinion Research Center
> [producer] ; Storrs, Conn. : Roper Public Opinion
> Research Center [distributor]

9.4F. Date of publication, distribution, etc.

9.4F1. Give the date of publication, distribution, etc., of a published file as instructed in 1.4F.

Ann Arbor, Mich. : University of Michigan, Institute for Social Research, 1968

Chicago : University of Chicago, 1961-1962

Richmond, Va. : Rhiannon Software, c1985

[United States : s.n., 198-]

9.4F2. Give the date of an unpublished computer file as instructed in 1.4F9.

9.4F3. Give any other useful dates (e.g., dates of collection of data) in a note (see 9.7B7).

9.5. PHYSICAL DESCRIPTION AREA[3]

Contents:
- 9.5A. Preliminary rule
- 9.5B. Extent of item (including specific material designation)
- 9.5C. Other physical details
- 9.5D. Dimensions
- 9.5E. Accompanying material

9.5A. Preliminary rule

9.5A1. Punctuation
For instructions on the use of spaces before and after prescribed punctuation, see 1.0C.
Precede this area by a full stop, space, dash, space or start a new paragraph.
Precede other physical details by a colon.
Precede dimensions by a semicolon.
Precede a statement of accompanying material by a plus sign.
Enclose physical details of accompanying material in parentheses.

---

3. Do not give a physical description for a computer file that is available only by remote access.

9.5B. Extent of item (including specific material designation)

9.5B1. Record the number of physical units of the carrier by giving the number of parts in arabic numerals and one of the terms listed below, as appropriate:

> computer cartridge
> computer cassette
> computer disk
> computer reel

1 computer disk

2 computer cassettes

1 computer reel

As new physical carriers are developed, for which none of these terms is appropriate, give the specific name of the physical carrier as concisely as possible, preferably qualified by the word "computer."

If the information is readily available and if desired, indicate the specific type of physical medium.

1 computer chip cartridge

1 computer tape cartridge

1 computer tape reel

1 computer laser optical disk

Optionally, if general material designations are used (see 9.1C), omit the word "computer" from the specific material designation.

Give a trade name or other specification in a note (see 9.7B1b).

9.5C. Other physical details

9.5C1. If the file is encoded to produce sound, give the abbreviation <u>sd.</u> If the file is encoded to display in two or more colours, give the abbreviation <u>col.</u>

    1 computer disk : col.

    1 computer chip cartridge : sd.

    1 computer disk cartridge : sd., col.

Give details of the requirements for the production of sound or the display of colour in a note (see 9.7B1b).

9.5C2. <u>Optionally</u>, give the following physical characteristics of disks, if readily available and if they are considered to be important:

> number of sides used
> recording density (e.g., single, double)
> sectoring

    1 computer disk : sd., col., single sided, single density, soft sectored

9.5D. Dimensions

9.5D1. Give the dimensions of the physical carrier as instructed below.

a) <u>Disks</u>. Give the diameter of the disk in inches, to the next 1/4 inch up.

    1 computer disk : col. ; 5 1/4 in.

b) <u>Cartridges</u>. Give, in inches to the next 1/4 inch up, the length of the edge of the cartridge that is to be inserted into the machine.

    1 computer chip cartridge ; 3 1/2 in.

c) <u>Cassettes</u>. Give the dimensions of the cassette if they are other than the standard dimensions (3 7/8 x 2 1/2 in.) in inches, to the next 1/8 inch up.

9.5E. Accompanying material

9.5E1. Record the details of accompanying material as instructed in 1.5E. [See Appendix to this draft revision.]

> 1 computer disk ; 5 1/4 in. + user's guide

> 1 computer disk : col. ; 5 1/4 in. + 1 v. (51 p. : ill. ; 20 cm.)

> 1 computer disk ; 5 1/4 in. + user manual
> and addendum
> > (Addendum is part of the manual)

> 1 computer cassette : col. + 1 sound cassette (20 min. : analog, stereo.)

> 1 computer disk ; 5 1/4 in. + demonstration disk + codebook

> 2 computer disks ; 5 1/4 in.
> Note: Second disk is back-up

> 1 computer cassette + 7 pamphlets

> 1 computer disk ; 5 1/4 in. + data disk + 1 v. (140 p. : ill. ; 10 cm.)

9.5E2. If no physical description is given (see footnote 3 at 9.5), give details of any accompanying material in a note (see 9.7B11).

9.6. SERIES AREA

> Contents:
> > 9.6A. Preliminary rule
> > 9.6B. Series statements

9.6A. Preliminary rule

9.6A1. Punctuation

For instructions on the use of spaces before and after prescribed punctuation, see 1.0C.

Precede this area by a full stop, space, dash, space.

Enclose each series statement (see 1.6J) in parentheses.

Precede parallel titles of series or subseries by an equals sign.

Precede other title information relating to a series or subseries by a colon.

Precede the first statement of responsibility relating to a series or subseries by a diagonal slash.

Precede subsequent statements of responsibility relating to a series or subseries by a semicolon.

Precede the ISSN of a series or subseries by a comma.

Precede the numbering within a series or subseries by a semicolon.

Precede the title of a subseries by a full stop.

9.6B. Series statements

9.6B1. Record each series statement as instructed in 1.6.

(Practicorp no-nonsense software)

(American national election study series ; no. 13)

(Series C. Machine-readable texts of Greek authors)

9.7. NOTE AREA

Contents:
9.7A. Preliminary rule
9.7B. Notes

9.7A. Preliminary rule

9.7A1. Punctuation

Precede each note by a full stop, space, dash, space <u>or</u> start a new paragraph for each.

Separate introductory wording from the main content of a note by a colon and a space.

9.7A2. In making notes, follow the instructions in 1.7A.

9.7B. Notes
   Make notes as set out in the following subrules and in the order given there.

9.7B1. Nature and scope and system requirements

9.7B1a. <u>Nature and scope</u>. Make notes on the nature or scope of the file unless it is apparent from the rest of the description.

   Game

   Word processor

   Combined time series analysis and graph plotting system

   Spread sheet, with word processing and graphic capabilities

9.7B1b. <u>System requirements.</u> Always make a note on the system requirements of the file if the information is readily available. Precede the note by <u>System requirements</u>. Give the following characteristics in the order in which they are listed below, each, other than the first, preceded by a semicolon:

   the make and model of the computer(s) on
      which the file is designed to run
   the amount of memory required
   the name of the operating system
   the software requirements (including the
      programming language)
   the kind and characteristics of any required
      or recommended peripherals

   System requirements: 48K RAM; Apple Disk II with
Controller; colour monitor
   (<u>File requires colour monitor for display</u>)

   System requirements: 48K RAM; DOS 3.3

   System requirements: 64K; colour card; 1 disk
drive

19

System requirements: Apple II, II+, or IIe; 48K; DOS 3.3; Applesoft in ROM

System requirements: 48K; DOS 3.3; Applesoft BASIC; some programs require game paddles

System requirements: IBM PC or IBM PC compatible; 128K; DOS 1.1 to DOS 2.1

9.7B1c. Mode of access. If a file is available only by remote access, always specify the mode of access.

Online access via AUSINET

Mode of access: Electronic mail using ARPA

9.7B2. Language and script. Give an indication of the language and/or script of the spoken or written content of a file unless this is apparent from the rest of the description.

In German

Greek language transcribed in medieval manuscript tradition

Do not record the programming language here (see 9.7B1b).

9.7B3. Source of title proper. Make notes on the source of the title proper.

Title from title screen

Title from "catalogue record" provided by the producer

Title from codebook

Title supplied in correspondence by creator of the file

Title supplied by cataloguer

9.7B4. Variations in title. Give titles borne by the item other than the title proper. If considered desirable, give a romanization of the title proper.

> Title on manual: Compu-math decimals

> Also known as: MAXLIK

Optionally, record a file name or data set name if it differs from the title proper. For a locally assigned file name or data set name, see 9.7B20.

> File name: CC.RIDER

9.7B5. Parallel titles and other title information. Give parallel titles and other title information not recorded in the title and statement of responsibility area if they are considered to be important.

9.7B6. Statements of responsibility. Give statements relating to collaborators, sponsors, etc., or to persons or bodies who have prepared or contributed to the production of the item if they are not named elsewhere in the description and are judged necessary to the bibliographic description.

> Data collected in collaboration with Christiane Klapisch, École pratique des hautes études, Paris

> Additional contributors to program: Eric Rosenfeld, Debra Spencer

> Simulation rev. and reprogrammed by John Smith for use in an online time-sharing environment

> "Personal bibliographic software" copyrighted by Victor Rosenberg

> Systems designer, Henry Letow ; sound, LF Acoustics

> User's guide by John Unger Zussman

9.7B7. Edition and history. Give the source of the edition statement if it is different from that of the title proper.

Edition statement from container label

Make notes on the edition being described and the history of the item.

Updated version of 1982 program

Give details of minor changes such as those listed in 9.2B4 if they are considered to be important.

Mnemonic tags substituted for numeric tags

Monochrome version recoded for colour

Cite other works upon which the item depends for its content.

Based on: Historiae / edited by H.S. Jones and J.E. Powell. Reprint of 1942 ed. Oxford : Clarendon Press, 1967-1970. 2 v.

Give the following dates and details about them if they are considered to be important to the understanding of the content, use, or nature of the file:

a) the date(s) covered by the content of a file;
b) the date(s) when data were collected;
c) the date(s) of accompanying material not described separately if they differ from those of the file being described.

New England sermons, 1790-1900

Program first issued in 1981

Data collected May-Aug. 1981

Manual dated 1983

Includes supplementary file dated 1981

9.7B8. File characteristics. Give important file

ke informal, additional, or partial contents notes
appropriate.

Contains information on all 50 states

Each record contains selected fields from the
cords with less than 2049 characters issued on
MARC tape v. 6, no. 5

. **Numbers borne by the item.** Give important num-
orne by the item other than ISBNs and ISSNs (see

APX-10050

. **Copy being described, library's holdings, and
restrictions on use.** Make notes on any peculiar-
and imperfections of the item being described
re considered to be important. If the library
t hold a complete set of a multipart item, give
s of the library's holdings. If desired, record
lly assigned file or data set name. If desired,
e date when the content of the file was copied
r transferred to, another source.

ocal data set name: RBBIT.1

opied June 1983

ibrary also holds back-up disk

cate if the file is not available to all users
catalogue or other list. If possible, word the
general terms.

le closed until Jan. 1990

stricted to scholarly use

"With" notes. If the description is of a sep-
titled part of an item lacking a collective
ake a note beginning <u>With:</u> and listing the
parately titled parts of the item in the order
they appear there.

th: Uncle Sam's jigsaw -- U.S. Constitution
r -- Scramble

characteristics that have not been included in the file
characteristics area.

Hierarchical file structure

Number of variables: 960

Number of routines: 102

File size varies

File size unknown

ASCII characters

Blocked BCDs, 40 records per block, 90 characters
per record

If a file consists of numerous parts and the numbering cannot be given succinctly and if the information
is considered to be important, give the number or
approximate number of records, statements, etc., in
each part.

File size: 520, 300, 280, 400, 320, 400, 500
records

File size: ca. 520, 300, 400, 320 statements

9.7B9. Publication, distribution, etc. Make notes on
publication, distribution, etc., details that are not
included in the publication, etc., area and are considered to be important.

Solely distributed by the Laboratory

User's manual distributed by the American
Political Science Association, Washington, D.C.

9.7B10. Physical description. Give important physical
details that cannot be included in the physical description area. When describing a file available by remote
access, give any physical details (e.g., colour, sound)
if they are readily available and considered important.

Stereo. sound

Second disk is back-up

Displays in red, yellow, and blue

9.7B11. Accompanying material. Give details of accompanying material not:

 a) mentioned in the physical description area (see 9.5E);
 or b) given a separate entry;
 or c) given a separate description according to the rules for multilevel description (see 13.6).

Accompanied by a series of 5 programs in PL/1, with assembler subroutines

Documentation entitled: 1980 census user's guide. Pts. I-II. Washington, D.C. : Supt. of Docs., 1982

9.7B12. Series. Make notes on series data that cannot be given in the series area.

Originally issued in series: European Community study series

9.7B13. Dissertations. If the file is a dissertation, make a note as instructed in 2.7B13.

Thesis (M.A.) -- University of Illinois at Urbana-Champaign, 1984

9.7B14. Audience. Make a brief note of the intended audience for, or the intellectual level of, a file if this information is stated in or on the item, its container, or accompanying material.

For ages 7-10

Intended audience: High school students

For use by qualified medical practitioners only

Designed for those with a p
analyzing spatial data (geogr
meteorologists, etc.)

9.7B16. Other formats. Make no
which the file has also been issu

Data also issued in printe

If the content of the file is
computer-readable version, indic

Issued also for IBM PC and

9.7B17. Summary. Give a brief
the purpose and content of the
of the description gives enough

Summary: Can be used to m
aggregate raw data in any m
assigning values to the coo
data points or data zones,
three types of map: contour

Summary: Responses of New
Harris study questionnaire
May 1969

Summary: Eight versions (
players. To survive, play(
destroy flying demons

Summary: A simulation of
the German invasion of Rus

9.7B18. Contents. Make a lis

Contents: 1. Idaho -- 2
4. Washington

Contents: Moby Dick --
Huckleberry Finn -- Scarl

Ma
when

r
L(

9.7B1
bers h
9.8B).

9.7B20
local
ities
that a
does n
detail
a loca
give t
from,

I

(

I

Indi
of the
note in

F

R

9.7B21.
arately
title, i
other se
in which

Wi
tut(

9.8. STANDARD NUMBER AND TERMS OF AVAILABILITY AREA

Contents:
9.8A. Preliminary rule
9.8B. Standard number
9.8C. Key-title
9.8D. Terms of availability
9.8E. Qualification

9.8A. Preliminary rule

9.8A1. Punctuation

For instructions on the use of spaces before and after prescribed punctuation, see 1.0C.

Precede this area by a full stop, space, dash, space or start a new paragraph.

Precede each repetition of this area by a full stop, space, dash, space.

Precede a key-title by an equals sign.

Precede terms of availability by a colon.

Enclose a qualification to the standard number or terms of availability in parentheses.

9.8B. Standard number

9.8B1. Give the International Standard Book Number (ISBN) or International Standard Serial Number (ISSN) assigned to a published file as instructed in 1.8B.

Give an ISBN or ISSN assigned to accompanying material.

ISBN 0-89138-111-2 (codebook)

9.8B2. Give any other number assigned to a file in a note (see 9.7B19).

9.8C. Key-title

9.8C1. Give the key-title of a serial file as instructed in 1.8C.

9.8D. Optional addition. Terms of availability

9.8D1. Give the terms on which an item is available as instructed in 1.8D.

27

$800.00

Free to universities and colleges, for hire to others

9.8E. Qualification

9.8E1. Add qualifications to the standard number and/ or terms of availability as instructed in 1.8E.

9.9. SUPPLEMENTARY ITEMS
Describe supplementary items as instructed in 1.9.

9.10. ITEMS MADE UP OF SEVERAL TYPES OF MATERIAL
Describe items made up of several types of material as instructed in 1.10.

Draft Revision of Rule
on Accompanying Material

1.5E. Accompanying material

1.5E1. Record details of accompanying material in one of
the following ways:

       a) make a separate entry;
_or_   b) make a multilevel description (see chapter 13);
_or_   c) make a note (see 1.7B11);

       Accompanied by "A demographic atlas of North-
       west Ireland" (39 p. : col. maps ; 36 cm.),
       previously published separately in 1956

       Teacher's guide (24 p.) by Robert Garry Shirts

       Accompanied by filmstrip: Mexico and Central
       America

_or_   d) record the name of the accompanying material at
       the end of the physical description;

       387 p. : ill. ; 27 p. + teacher's notes

       32 p. : col. ill. ; 28 cm. + maps

       271 p. : ill. ; 21 cm. + atlas

       1 stereograph reel (12 double fr.) : col. +
       booklet

       1 score (32 p.) ; 26 cm. + sound cassettes

> 1 computer disk ; 5 1/4 in. + demonstration
> disk + user's notes

or   e) record the number of physical units of the
     accompanying material in arabic numerals and
     the specific material designation as specified
     in the following chapters (but use "v." for
     items for which chapter 2 specifies "p.")

> 387 p. : ill. ; 27 cm. + 1 v.

> 32 p. : col. ill. ; 28 cm. + 3 maps

> 40 slides : col. + 1 sound disc

Optional addition. If method e is used and if more
detail is desired, add the physical description of the accompanying material as specified in the following chapters.

> 1 stereograph reel (12 double fr.) : col. + 1 v.
> (12 p. : ill. ; 18 cm.)

> 1 filmstrip (70 fr.) : sd., col. ; 35 mm. + 1 v.
> (39 p. ; 22 cm.)

> 271 p. : ill. ; 21 cm. + 1 v. (95 p. : 85 col.
> maps ; 32 cm.)